Frances Turnbull

Published by Musicaliti® Publishers
575 Tonge Moor Road, Bolton, BL2 3BN

Copyright © 2016 Musicaliti
ISBN 978-1-907935-73-2

All rights reserved. No part of this publication may be reproduced, stored in a retrieval system, or transmitted by any means, mechanical, photocopying, recording or otherwise, without the prior permission of the copyright holder.

Index of Songs

Circle Right	15
Circle to the Left	12
G-Scale	19
Mummy Loves	14
Old King Glory	13
Oranges and Lemons	16
Phoebe Phoebe	10
Rabbit Run	18
Skip to my Lou	17
The Little Bells	9
There was a jolly miller	11

Guitar Basics

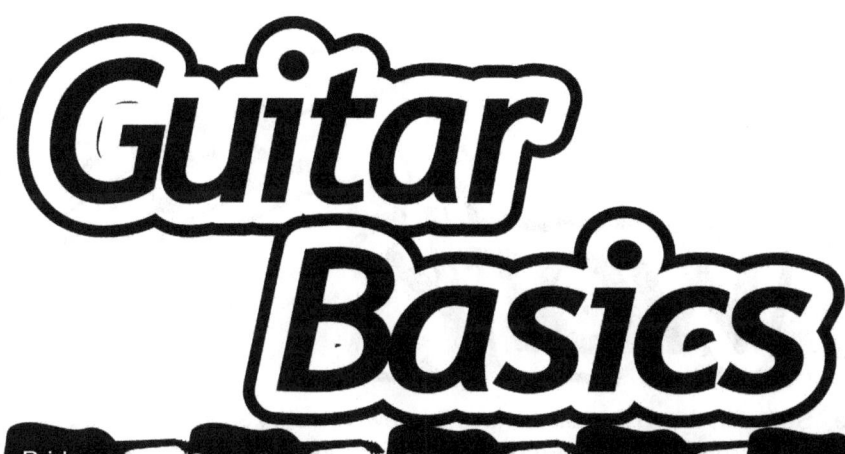

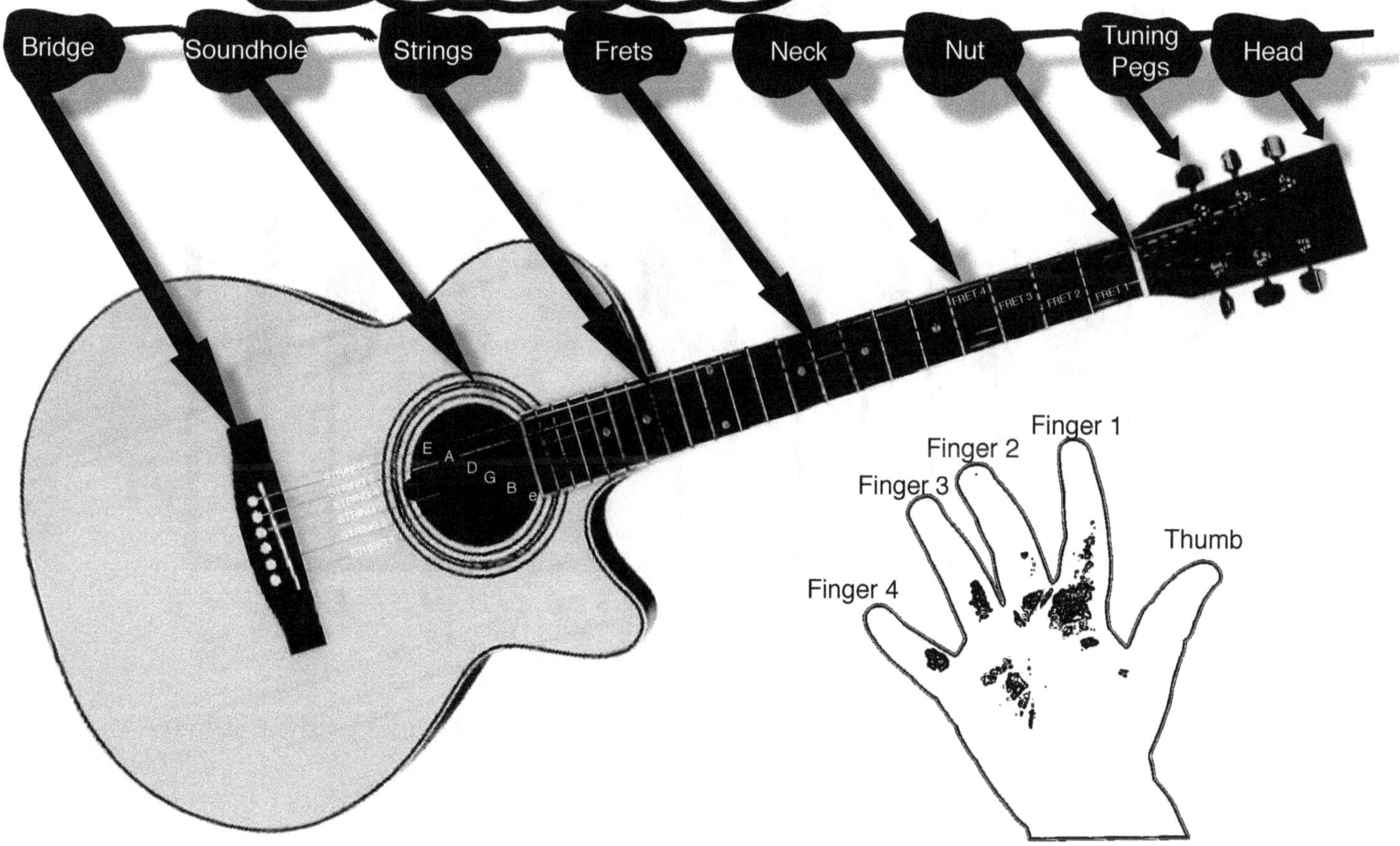

Bridge
Soundhole
Strings
Frets
Neck
Nut
Tuning Pegs
Head
FRET 4
FRET 3
FRET 2
FRET 1
E
A
D
G
B
e
Finger 1
Finger 2
Finger 3
Finger 4
Thumb

2
1
4

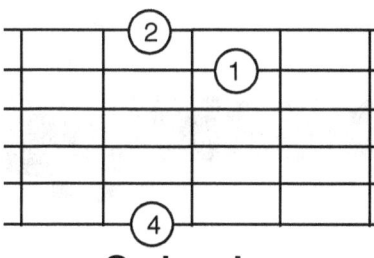

G chord

Guitar can be used to play tunes or **melodies** (one or a few notes at a time) or to accompany songs being sung - by playing all the strings with your fingers in the shape of a chord. The songs in this book are all in the chord of G. This means that you can play the G chord and sing along to the songs, or play the tune - it is a great skill to be able to do both! You could even have a guitar friend play the chord while you play the melody (tune) or the other way around! These pictures show the chords that we have used in this book. The numbers in circles show which finger to use!

3
2
1

C chord

1
3
2

D chord

1
2

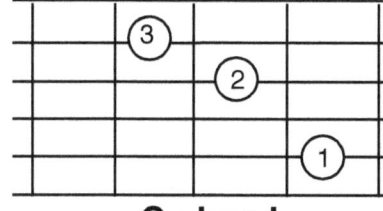

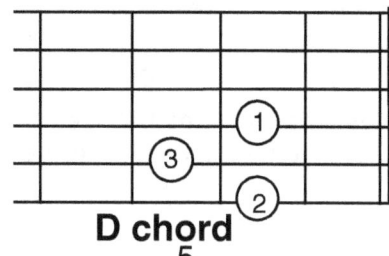

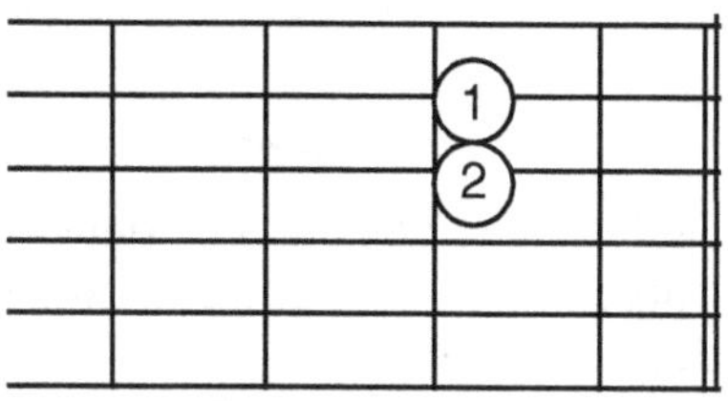

Em chord

How the notes work

The songs in this book are written in the **G scale**. Songs in the **green book** have the fewest notes as you get used to playing the notes of songs on the guitar, with more notes in **pink book**, **yellow book**, **blue book** and **orange book**.

The notes in a G scale are: **G, A, B, C, D, E, F#**. On a **piano**, they look like this:

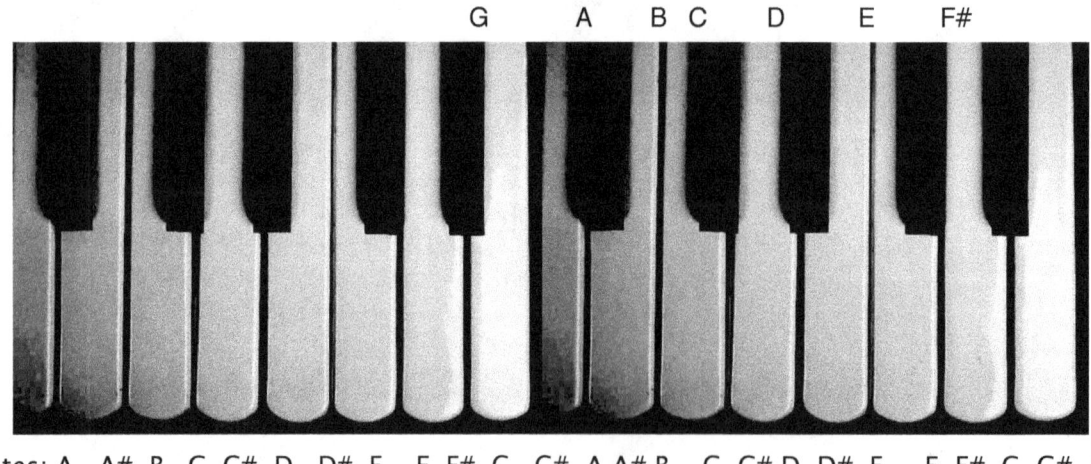

Music notes: A A#/Bb B C C#/Db D D#/Eb E F F#/Gb G G#/Ab A A#/Bb B C C#/Db D D#/Eb E F F#/Gb G G#/Ab A

On a **guitar**, they look like this:
(guitar strings start with different notes/letters, and this picture shows the notes on the E string)

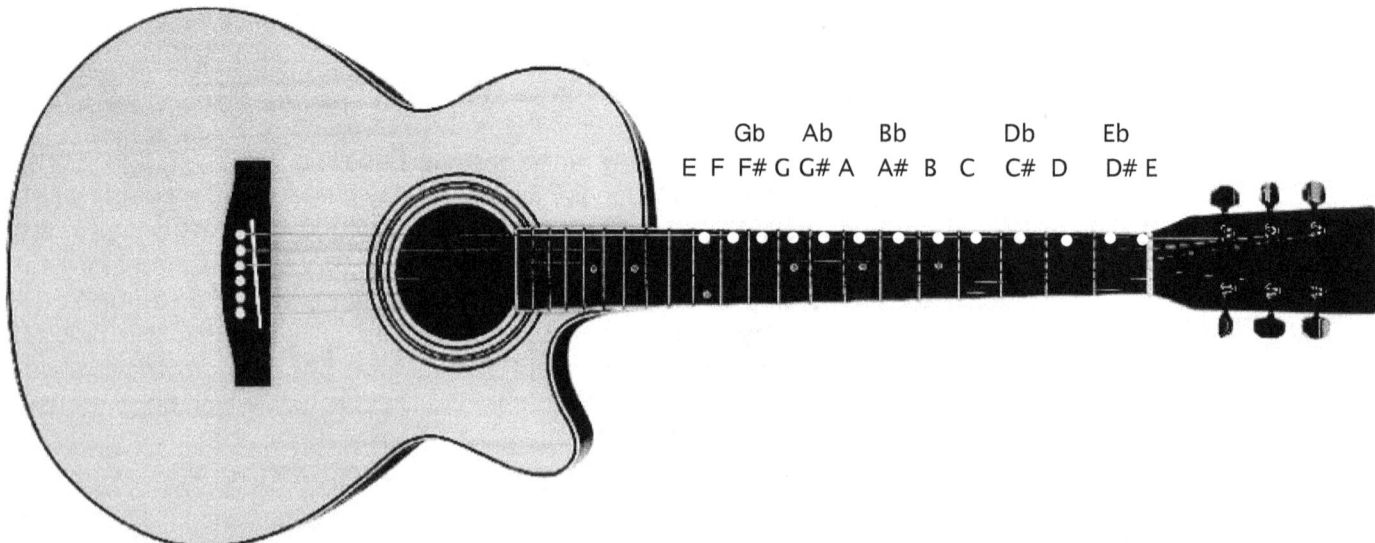

Scales have set gaps in between the notes, and the gaps between these notes determine when the black notes, or sharps and flats (also called accidentals) are used. Accidentals can be sharp (#) or flat (b), depending on the scale.

How the beats work

It's easy to focus on only playing the right notes, but we need to get the **long and short** beats right, too. It can be tricky to work out until we know what the lines and holes in the notes mean, so we can use **movement words** to remember how the beats sound. That way, you could say the movement words instead of the song words to remember how long to play the note!

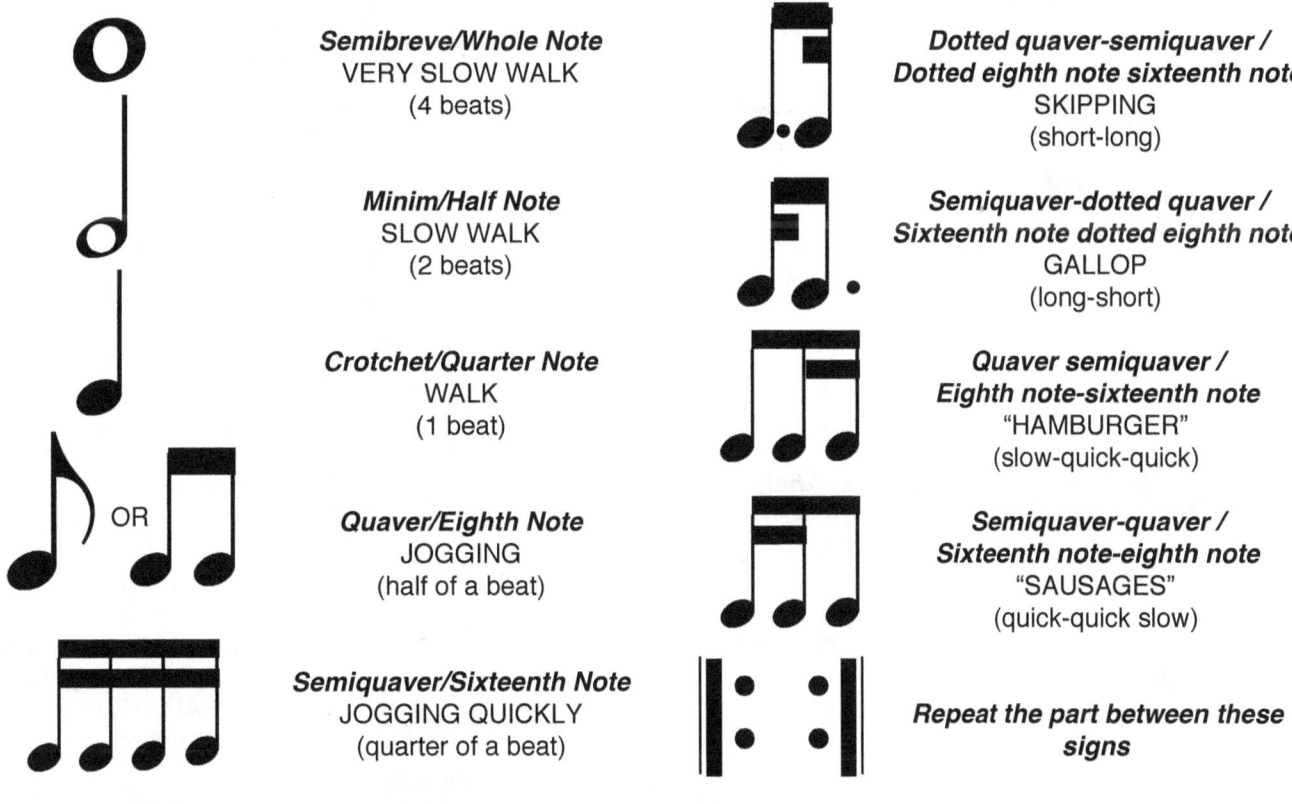

- **Semibreve/Whole Note** — VERY SLOW WALK (4 beats)
- **Minim/Half Note** — SLOW WALK (2 beats)
- **Crotchet/Quarter Note** — WALK (1 beat)
- **Quaver/Eighth Note** — JOGGING (half of a beat)
- **Semiquaver/Sixteenth Note** — JOGGING QUICKLY (quarter of a beat)
- **Dotted quaver-semiquaver / Dotted eighth note sixteenth note** — SKIPPING (short-long)
- **Semiquaver-dotted quaver / Sixteenth note dotted eighth note** — GALLOP (long-short)
- **Quaver semiquaver / Eighth note-sixteenth note** — "HAMBURGER" (slow-quick-quick)
- **Semiquaver-quaver / Sixteenth note-eighth note** — "SAUSAGES" (quick-quick slow)
- **Repeat the part between these signs**

For example, if we sang the movement rhythms to "This Old Man", we would have:

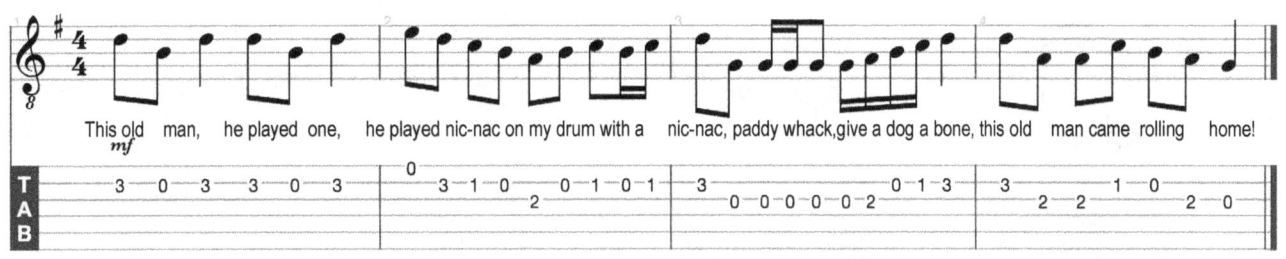

jogging - walk - jogging - walk   jogging-jogging-jogging-hamburger   jogging-sausages-running quickly-walk   jogging - jogging - jogging - walk

Give it a try before singing the songs!

7

Blue Songs

These pages introduce songs with 5 notes, and the different lengths of beats used:

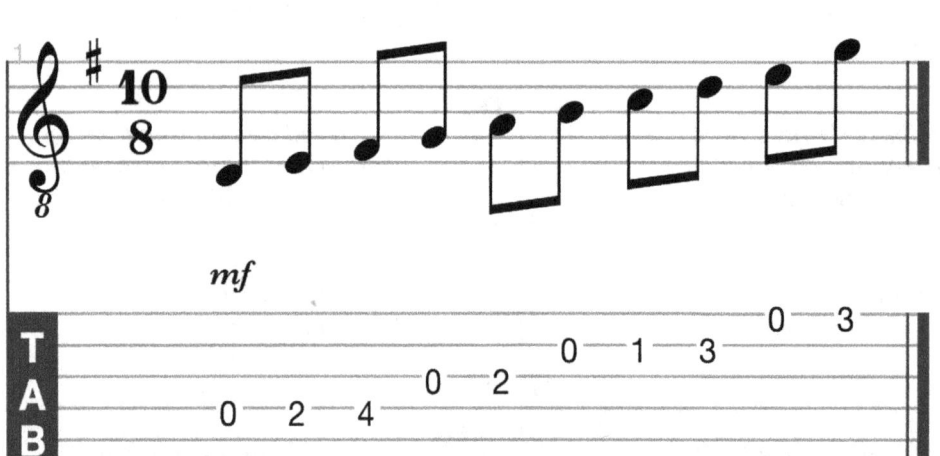

E is on the 1st open string
D is on the 2nd string, 3rd fret
C is on the 2nd string, 1st fret
B is on the 2nd open string
A is on the 3rd string, 2nd fret
G is on the 3rd open string
F# is on the 4th string, 4th fret
E is on the 4th string, 2nd fret
D is on the 4th open string

1st string
2nd string
3rd string
4th string
5th string
6th string

Semibreve/Whole Note
VERY SLOW WALK
(4 beats)

Minim/Half Note
SLOW WALK
(2 beats)

Crotchet/Quarter Note
WALK
(1 beat)

Quaver/Eighth Note
JOGGING
(half of a beat)

Semiquaver/Sixteenth Note
JOGGING QUICKLY
(quarter of a beat)

**Dotted quaver-semiquaver /
Dotted eighth note sixteenth note**
SKIPPING
(short-long)

**Semiquaver-dotted quaver /
Sixteenth note dotted eighth note**
GALLOP
(long-short)

**Quaver semiquaver /
Eighth note-sixteenth note**
"HAMBURGER"
(slow-quick-quick)

**Semiquaver-quaver /
Sixteenth note-eighth note**
"SAUSAGES"
(quick-quick slow)

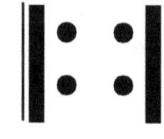

Repeat the part between these signs

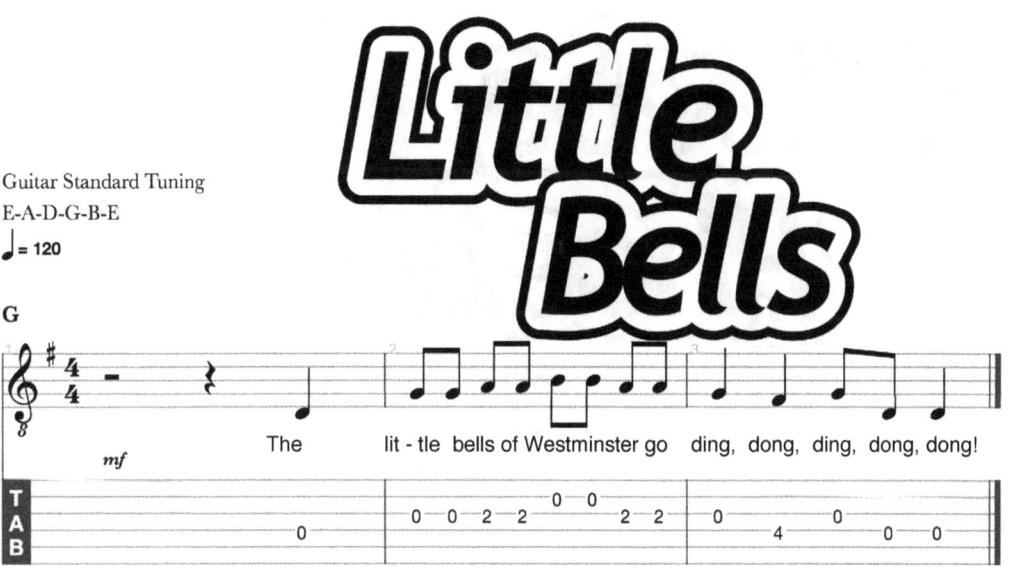

Little Bells

Guitar Standard Tuning
E-A-D-G-B-E
♩= 120

Traditional

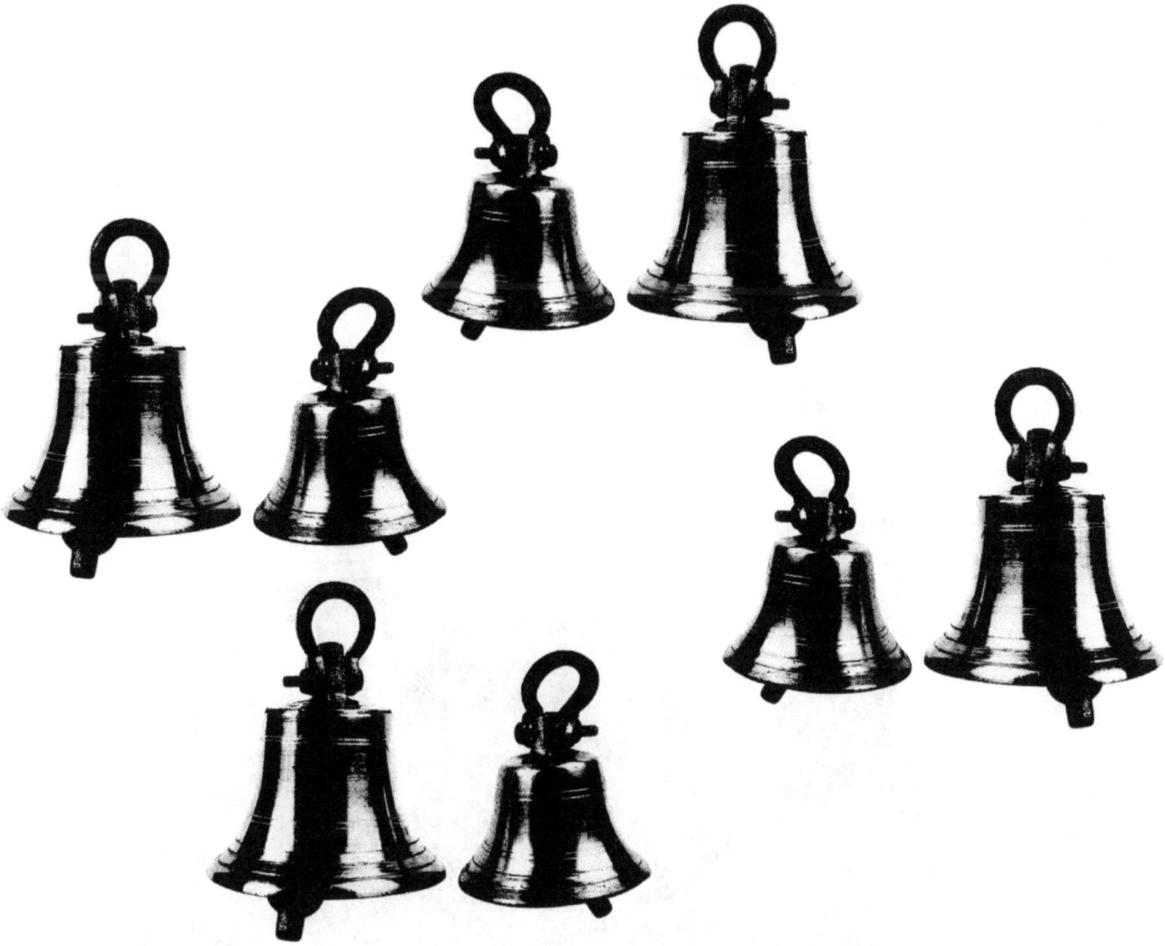

G
mf
The lit - tle bells of Westminster go ding, dong, ding, dong, dong!
T
A
B
0
0 0 2 2 0 0 2 2
0 4 0 0 0

Watch Out!

B
A
G
F#
D

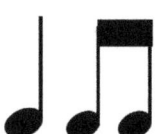

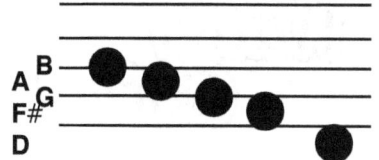

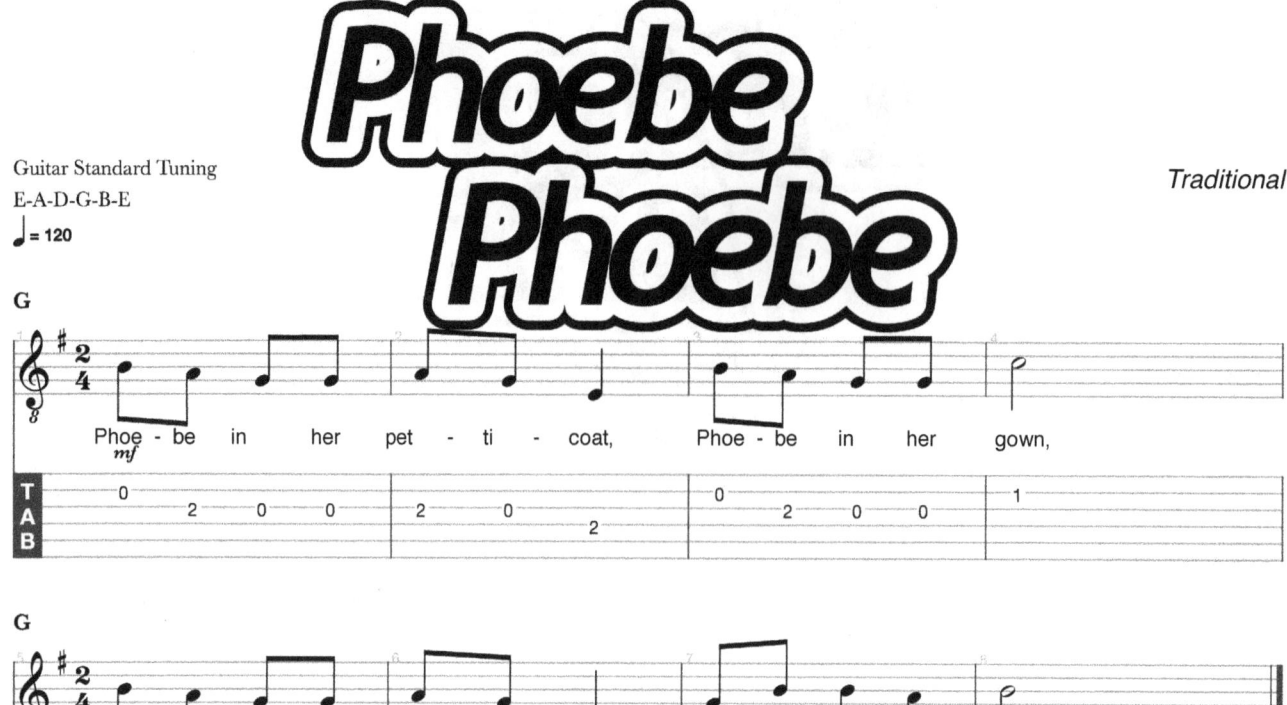

Phoebe Phoebe

Guitar Standard Tuning
E-A-D-G-B-E
♩ = 120

Traditional

G

Phoe - be in her pet - ti - coat, Phoe - be in her gown,

G

Phoe - be in her pet - ti - coat, go - ing down to town!

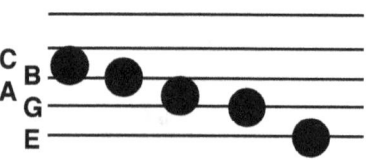

Circle to the Left

Guitar Standard Tuning
E-A-D-G-B-E
♩ = 100

Traditional

Cir - cle to the left, old brass wa - gon, cir - cle to the left, old brass wa - gon,

Cir - cle to the left, old brass wa - gon, you're the one my dar - ling!

Next verses:

Circle to the right, old brass wagon
Circle to the right, old brass wagon
Circle to the right, old brass wagon
You're the one my darling

Everybody down, old brass wagon
Everybody up, old brass wagon
Everybody down, old brass wagon
You're the one my darling

Everybody in, old brass wagon
Everybody out, old brass wagon
Everybody in, old brass wagon
You're the one my darling

  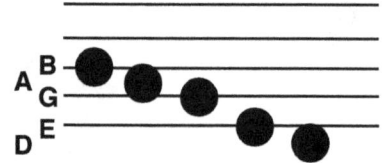

Guitar Standard Tuning
E-A-D-G-B-E
♩ = 120

Traditional

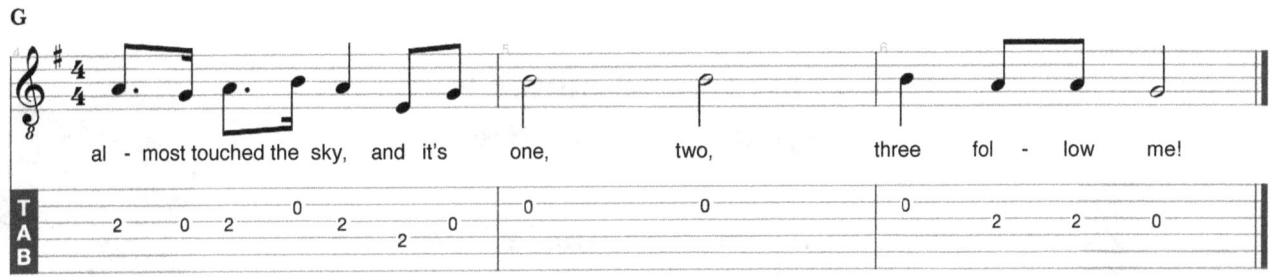

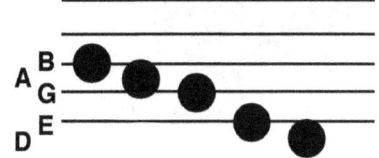

Guitar Standard Tuning
E-A-D-G-B-E
♩ = 120

Traditional

Mum - my loves and dad - dy loves and every - bo - dy loves lit - tle ba - by

Next verses:

Brother loves and sister loves and
Everybody loves little baby

Auntie loves and uncle loves and
Everybody loves little baby

Nanna loves and grandad loves and
Everybody loves little baby

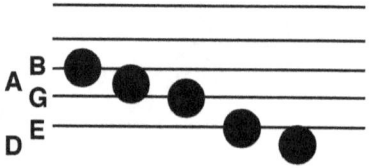

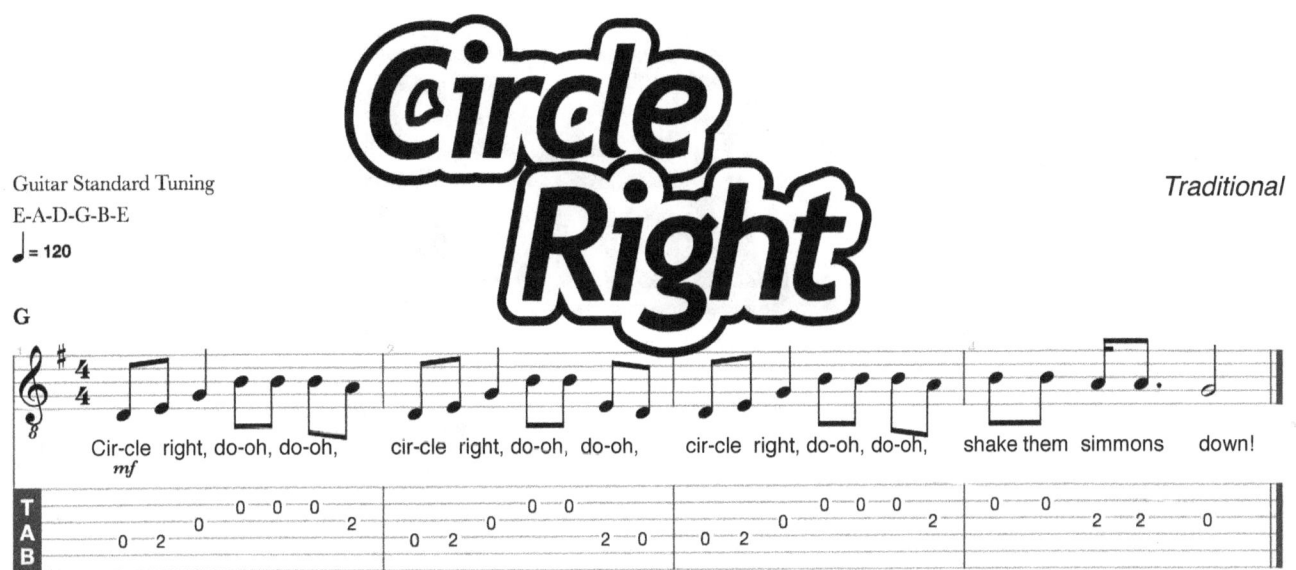

Guitar Standard Tuning
E-A-D-G-B-E
♩ = 120

Traditional

G

Cir-cle right, do-oh, do-oh, cir-cle right, do-oh, do-oh, cir-cle right, do-oh, do-oh, shake them simmons down!

Next verses:

Circle right, do-oh, do-oh
Circle right, do-oh, do-oh
Circle right, do-oh, do-oh
Shake them simmons down

Do-se-do, do-oh, do-oh
Do-se-do, do-oh, do-oh
Do-se-do, do-oh, do-oh
Shake them simmons down

Swing your partner, do-oh, do-oh
Swing your partner, do-oh, do-oh
Swing your partner, do-oh, do-oh
Shake them simmons down

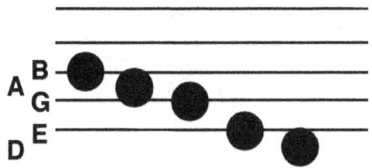

Oranges and Lemons

Guitar Standard Tuning
E-A-D-G-B-E
♩ = 110

Traditional

Oranges and le - mons, say the bells of Saint Cle - mens, you owe me two far-thing say the bells of Saint Mar - tins!

Next verse:

When will you pay me?
Say the bells of Old Bailey
When I grown rich
Say the bells of Shoreditch
When will that be?
Say the bells of Stepney
I do not know
Says the great bell of Bow

Skip to my Lou

Guitar Standard Tuning
E-A-D-G-B-E
♩= 120

Traditional

Skip, skip, skip to my Lou, skip, skip, skip to my Lou, skip, skip, skip to my Lou, Skip to my Lou, my dar - ling!
mf

Next verse:

Fly in the buttermilk, shoo fly shoo
Fly in the buttermilk, shoo fly shoo
Fly in the buttermilk, shoo fly shoo
Skip to my Lou, my darling

Cat's in the cream jar, what'll I do
Cat's in the cream jar, what'll I do
Cat's in the cream jar, what'll I do
Skip to my Lou, my darling

Dad's old hat got torn in two
Dad's old hat got torn in two
Dad's old hat got torn in two
Skip to my Lou, my darling

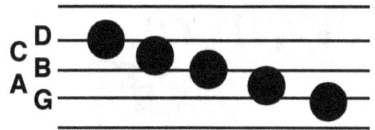

Rabbit Run

Guitar Standard Tuning
E-A-D-G-B-E
♩ = 120

Traditional

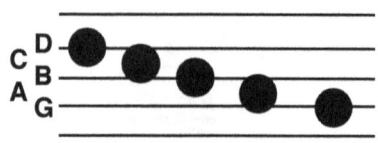

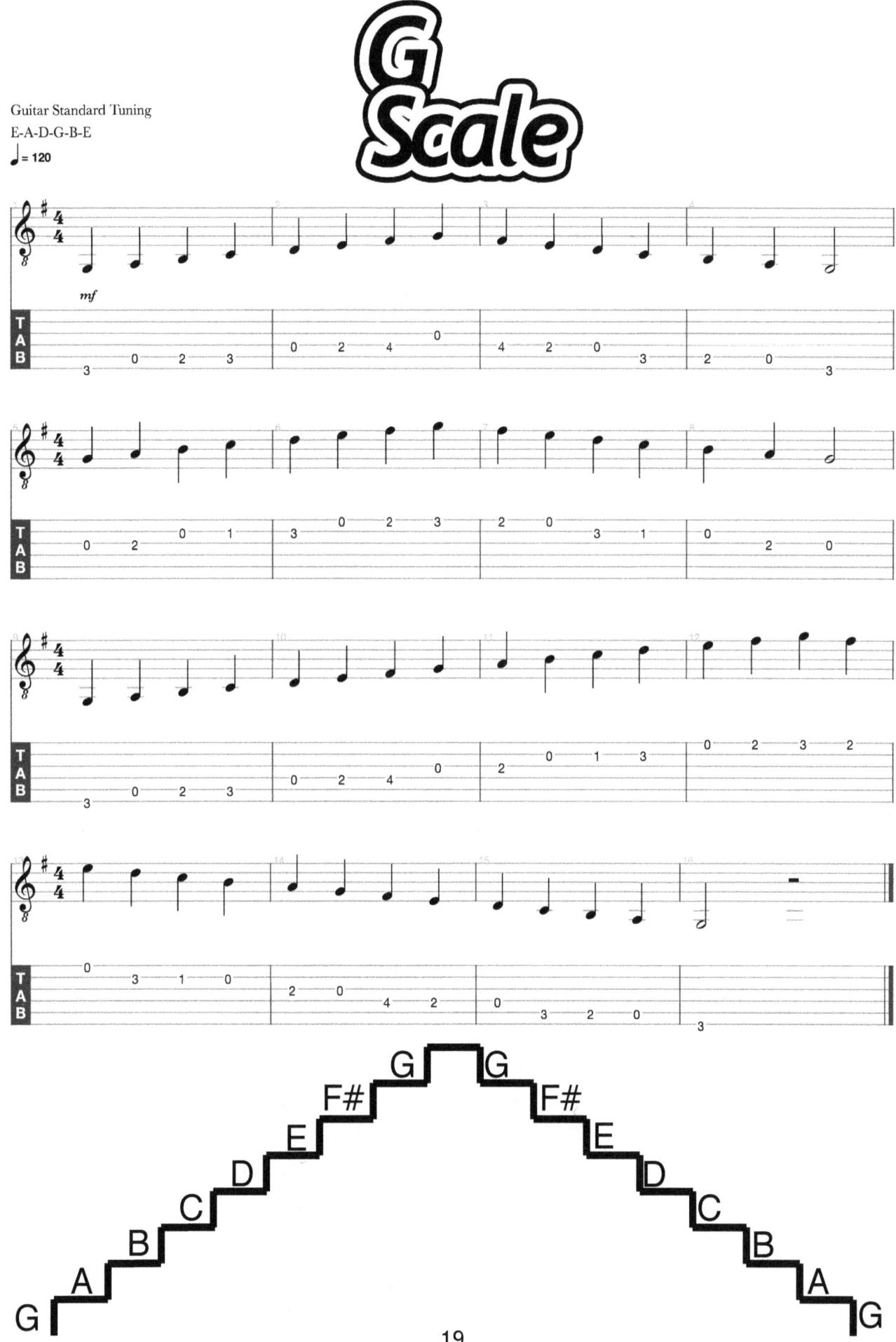

ABOUT THE AUTHOR

Frances has presented early years music sessions in a variety of settings since 2006, after training as a secondary mathematics and science teacher. She is fascinated by research into the health, educational and developmental benefits of music. Not content with being involved with children's music alone, she directs a local community choir, the Warblers.

AVAILABLE TITLES:

Musicaliti Nursery: Round and Round is a full-colour, illustrated book of well known children's songs for children. Each song includes music rhythms to which children can clap, tap, walk and sing.
ISBN: 978-1-907-935-008

Musicaliti Nursery Series: Magical Musical Kingdom is a full-colour, teaching series of well known and original children's songs with a royal element. Sessions include suggested instruments and activities, with an optional CD of music to purchase or download.
ISBN: 978-1-907-935-152

Musicaliti Nursery Series: Sharks, Fish, Shells is a full-colour, teaching series of well known and original children's songs with a fishy element. Sessions include suggested instruments and activities, with an optional CD of music to purchase or download.
ISBN: 978-1-907-935-169

Musicaliti Nursery Series: Yum, Yum, Yum! is a full-colour, teaching series of well known and original children's songs with a foody element. Sessions include suggested instruments and activities, with an optional CD of music to purchase or download.
ISBN: 978-1-907-935-206

Musicaliti Music Gone Wild is a full-colour, teaching series of well known and original children's songs with an animal element. Using ukulele instruction and chords, play along with your favourite animal songs today!

ISBN: 978-1-907-935-688

Musicaliti Goodies for Guitar is a full-colour, teaching series of well known and original children's songs for beginner guitar. With 90 songs both familiar and unfamiliar, this book covers songs in the scale of G, providing music notation, tablature and guitar chords for accompaniment.
ISBN: 978-1-907-935-206

FORTHCOMING TITLES:

Musicaliti Nursery Series: Balloons, Candles, Cake is a full-colour, teaching series of well known and original children's songs with a party element. Sessions include suggested instruments and activities, with an optional CD of music to purchase or download.
ISBN: 978-1-907-935-190

Musicaliti Nursery Series: Car, bike, plane is a full-colour, teaching series of well known and original children's songs with a transport element. Sessions include suggested instruments and activities, with an optional CD of music to purchase or download.

ISBN: 978-1-907-935-213

Follow Musicaliti **NOW on FaceBook, LInkedIn, ReverbNation, SoundCloud, Twitter and YouTube!**

www.ingramcontent.com/pod-product-compliance
Lightning Source LLC
Chambersburg PA
CBHW081504040426
42446CB00016B/3398